The Fun Bus

Written by Jill Eggleton
Illustrated by Jan van der Voo

Rigby

Mr. Bigelow is a bus driver.
He drives a blue bus
up and down the town.

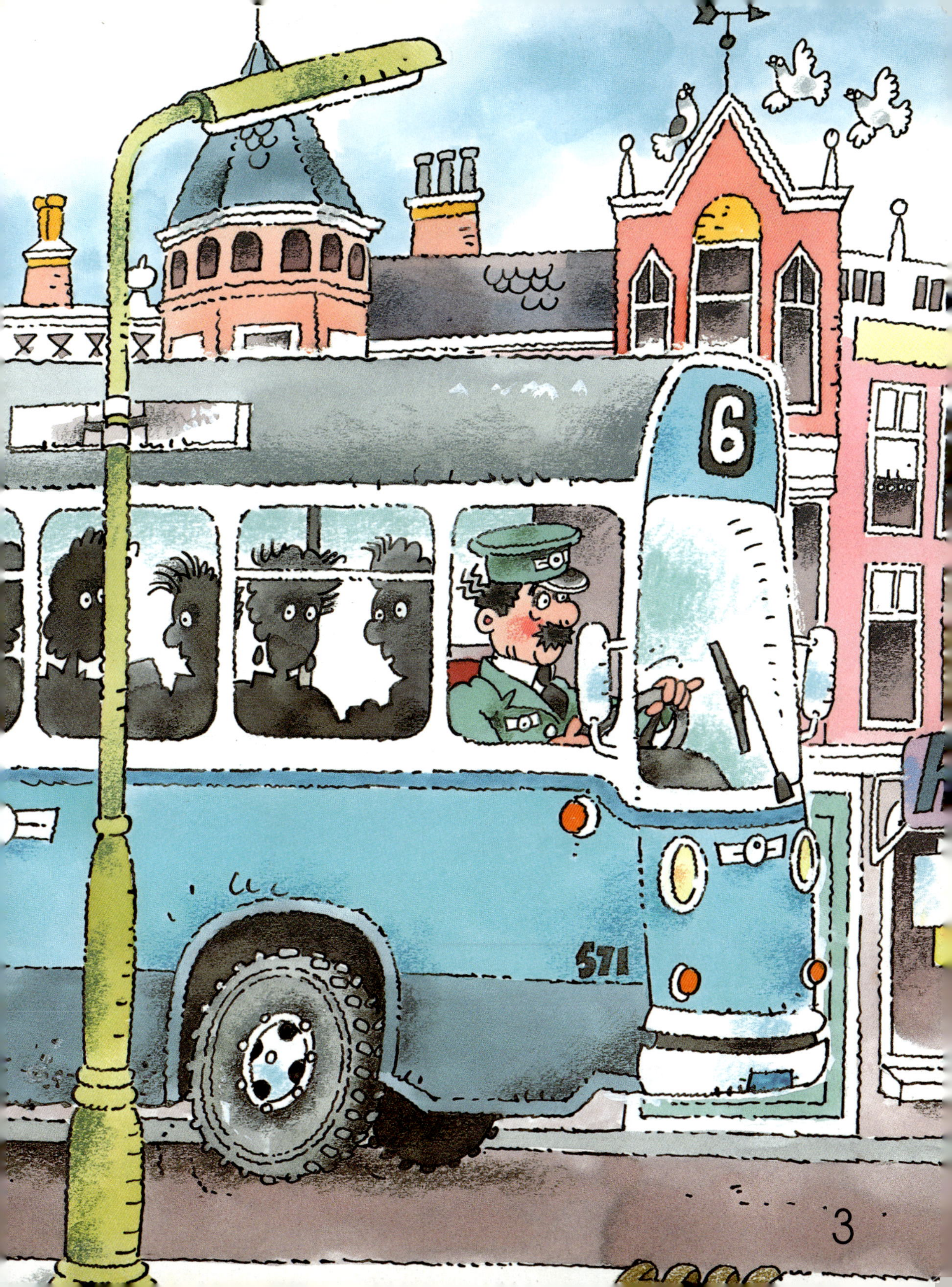
6
571

A girl with a box
got on Mr. Bigelow's bus.
"What is in that box?"
said Mr. Bigelow.

"Just a rooster," said the girl.
She opened the box
and out flew the rooster.

5

The people on the bus sang:
"There's a rooster on the bus!
There's a rooster on the bus!
We have never, ever, ever
seen a rooster on a bus!"

And they clapped their hands
and stamped their feet
and jiggled and wiggled
to the beat, beat, beat!

Mr. Bigelow said,
"I won't, I won't,
I won't have a fuss!
Take that rooster off my bus!"

A boy with a cage got on Mr. Bigelow's bus. "What is in that cage?" said Mr. Bigelow.

"Just a parrot," said the boy.
He opened the cage
and out flew the parrot.

The people on the bus sang:
"There's a parrot on the bus!
There's a parrot on the bus!
We have never, ever, ever
seen a parrot on a bus!"

And they clapped their hands
and stamped their feet
and *jiggled* and *wiggled*
to the beat, beat, beat!

Mr. Bigelow said,
"I won't I won't,
I won't have a fuss!
Take that parrot off my bus!"

11

A man with a basket got on Mr. Bigelow's bus. "What is in that basket?" said Mr. Bigelow.

"Just a peacock," said the man.
He opened the basket
and out flew the peacock.

The people on the bus sang:
"There's a peacock on the bus!
There's a peacock on the bus!
We have never, ever, ever
seen a peacock on a bus!"

And they clapped their hands
and stamped their feet
and jiggled and wiggled
to the beat, beat, beat!

Mr. Bigelow said,
"I won't, I won't,
I won't have a fuss!
Take that peacock off my bus!"

15

Mr. Bigelow went home.
"What's the matter?"
said Mrs. Bigelow.
"A rooster and a parrot
and a peacock got on my bus,
and the people made
a **terrible** fuss!"
said Mr. Bigelow.

"What fun!" said Mrs. Bigelow.
"I want to be a bus driver, too."

HOOL FOR BUS DRIVERS

So Mrs. Bigelow went to a school for bus drivers.

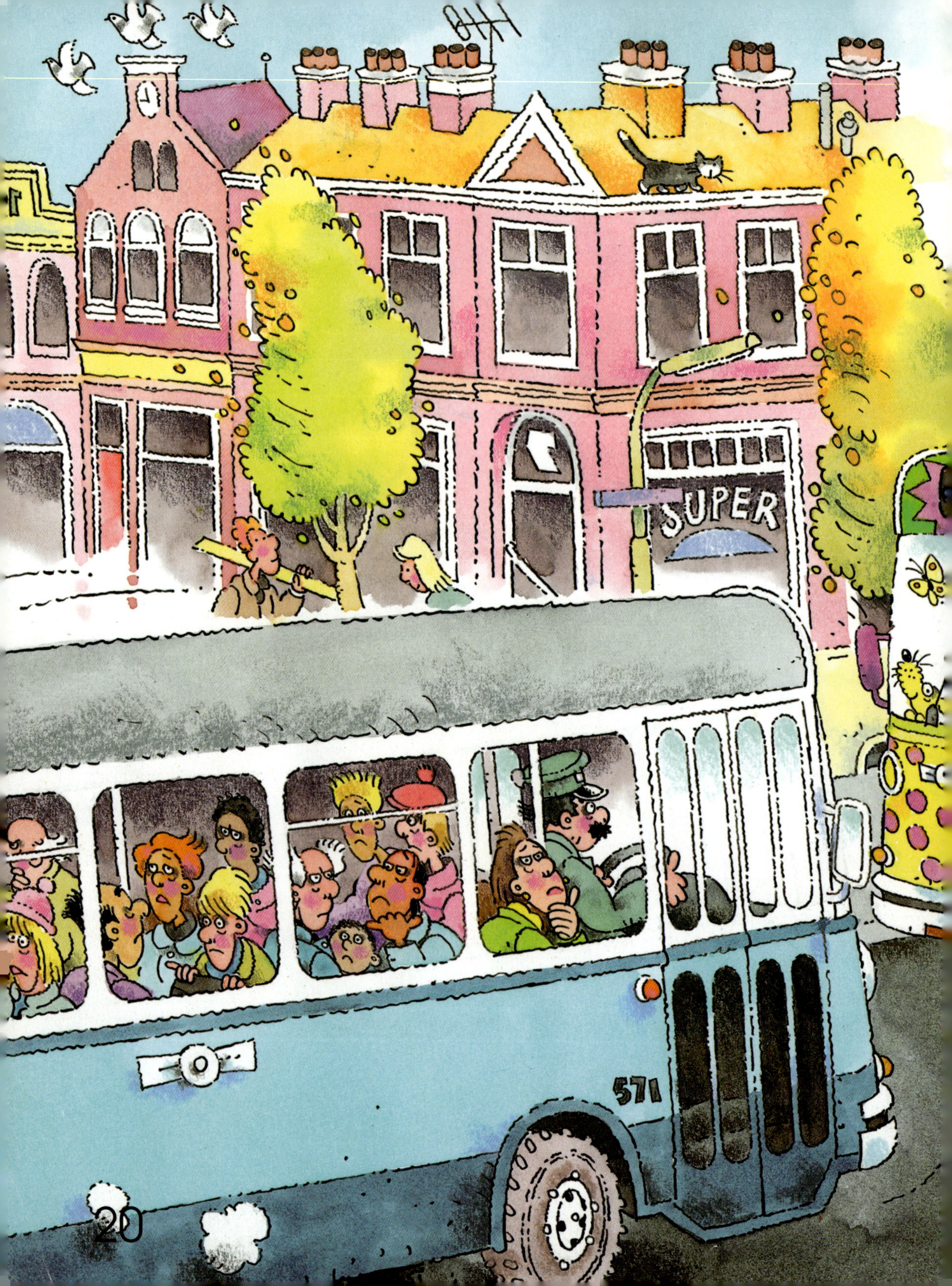
SUPER
571

Now Mrs. Bigelow drives a bus.
It is purple and yellow
and green.
It is called **"The Fun Bus."**

And the people on Mrs. Bigelow's bus clap their hands . . .

and stamp their feet
and *jiggle* and *wiggle*
to the beat, beat, beat!

Guide Notes

Title: The Fun Bus
Stage: Early

Genre: Fiction
Approach: Shared Reading
Processes: Thinking Critically, Exploring Language, Processing Information
Written and Visual Focus: Font Size

THINKING CRITICALLY
(sample questions)
- What do you think this story could be about?
- Discuss the cover and title. Do you think this story is going to be true or not true?
- Look at page 4. How do you think Mr. Bigelow feels about the rooster on his bus?
- Look at page 8. Why do you think the boy would be bringing a parrot onto the bus?
- Look at pages16-17. How do you think Mr. Bigelow feels? If you were Mr. Bigelow, what would you do?
- Why do you think Mrs. Bigelow went to bus driving school?
- What do you think she would learn at bus driving school?
- If you had to catch a bus, which one would you choose? Why?

EXPLORING LANGUAGE

Terminology
Title, cover, illustrations, author, illustrator

Vocabulary
Interest words: clapped, stamped, jiggled, wiggled, beat, terrible, fuss

Print Conventions
Captial letter for sentence beginnings and names (**M**r. **B**igelow, **M**rs. **B**igelow), periods, exclamation marks, quotation marks, commas